5 MINUTES

OF DAILY

VISUALISATION

Learn secrets to attract wealth, health, and happiness to create your destiny with the power of imagination.

GYAN S NARAYAN

Thanks for purchasing the book!

Scan QR code to get your Gift!

Table of Contents

Chapter 1

Introduction

To accomplish great things, we must not only act, but also dream; not only plan, but also believe

-Anatole France

People say that one should not look back on life; life is meant to move forward. This is very true; I am also a true believer of this idea. Everyone in his life will experience ups and downs; life is meant to be like that. It is like the graphical representation of a heartbeat, which is a curved line moving up, then down, and then moving up.

The curve becomes straight only when there is no life. So, for life to exist, the curve of the circumstances of our life must be both up and down. We may never have explored that the curve of the circumstances of life are always on an upward path. If I say this, I will contradict what has been said for ages: man is governed by destiny.

I used to entertain this notion, but now I totally deny it. I was told since childhood that every human being in this universe has a limitation. One is bound by destiny: you will achieve anything great in life only if it is your fate. God has carved a specific future for everyone; and it's true for me as well. Although my parents always encouraged me to do my best and achieve the most in life, we all know that our thoughts and beliefs are the average of the five people surrounding us.

My parents told me that there is no such term as fate, but the words of friends and relatives affect our minds. Now I believe that I am the victim of fabricated beliefs. In my schooling days, some students used to get high marks and earn top rank in class. They enjoyed the blessings of the teachers. In every subject, these so-called bright students used to score the higher marks and would earn great appreciation from the school community.

In fact, the best students' photographs would be published in the school magazine, which was published quarterly. My photograph was never published in the school magazine, so I grew up with the belief that I was a mediocre student. With every passing day, my belief got stronger and stronger. I felt myself being pushed back.

Life is like the sea; it will keep you near the shore with its waves if you are not strong enough to venture farther in. If your belief is not strong, you will not give yourself over to the circumstances. Just like the waves of water pushing you out to sea, you will find yourself out of the race of life. Writing these lines has brought tears to my eyes. I realize that all the beliefs about myself were my own created thoughts.

I kept on diminishing myself; with each passing day and the glory of my classmates who stood first, second, and third in class, I started comparing myself to the brightest students of the class. I started developing the belief that these students were more outspoken with the teachers, and they were the first to solve any questions on any subject.

These thoughts became true in the end. I felt neglected seeing how the teachers appreciated those students for solving the questions first. Today, when I look back, I laugh at myself. With negative thoughts, I made myself small. Why did this happen? Let me tell you. As two brothers, both of us gained admission to different schools for kindergarten. When I was admitted, I was very excited to join the school. In fact, I found a good bunch of friends to play with on the first day of admission. I was joyous on the inside, and my teachers liked my innocence. I got good attention in school. My teachers gave me the proper handholding.

I vividly remember that the teachers proactively helped me. They developed a lot of interest in me, and I felt motivated because of it. Most of the time, I would raise my hand to answer questions first. The teachers started to acknowledge my proactive attitude, and they appreciated me. Many a time, I set as an example for the other students. Being the first to finish the classwork, I earned the opportunity to be the class monitor. To designate a student as monitor was an "incentive tool" that teachers would use to motivate the students.

This kept me on cloud nine; the aftereffect was that I became the pride of my parents. I remember that my father was called to hoist flag at school while I stood by, first in the class. I clearly remember his face: his son had made him proud. Being a guest at the flag hoisting ceremony was a proud moment for my father. These activities gave me confidence in school as well as at home. I became the darling of my teacher, even though I was notorious — something I will reveal in upcoming lines.

At home, I could flawlessly execute my homework. I would only need a little guidance from my father. Every day was a bright one for me as I continued to enjoy the company of my friends. In a very short span of time, I became their leader; they followed me in any activity I chose. I had a few gangs of my best buddies; they were always with me during recess and sports. In simple words, I used to enjoy myself a lot; today I can very well say that those were my "Golden Days".

I was in this school until grade three. There was a reason. As two brothers, the elder was studying in a different school in a five-days-a-week program. However, my school was six days a week. Because of this, Father made the decision to admit me to my brother's school eventually to have a good family life, where the whole family could enjoy the weekend together.

It was a very good move on my father's part. Had I been in his place, I would have also done the same thing for my kids. But being a child — the blue-eyed boy of the teachers and the leader of my best buddies — I felt a shock. I thought that my created nest was going to be destroyed. Feelings of sadness started cropping up. I did not want to leave my friends and nor did my friends want to leave my company. I clearly remember the day when I broke the news that I would have to leave the school to go to my brother's school; all my friends were upset.

Suddenly, there was silence among my friends, and everyone felt sad. Yes, they had every reason for their less than sanguine feelings because they felt their leader, their jolly friend, would be leaving them. I recall that every day during recess period, as friends, we would share snacks prepared by our mothers. We could taste various foods, and the joy of sharing was enormous. I remember when my father came to pick me up from school one day; all my fellow friends encircled him and kept firing questions as to why he was taking their friend out of school. They literally pleaded with Father to take back his decision of getting me admitted in another school.

Those all friends were innocent kids; they could not see the bigger picture...the one my father had seen for me. People used to say that my brother's school was one of the best in the locality. Getting admission there was tough, and many students had great success after leaving. But life had to move forward, and Father filled out the admission form for class three in my brother's school.

My father was called for an interview. The funniest part came on the day of interview; I still remember it. I am sure you will laugh at my innocence. It so happened that when my turn came, there was a bell sound from the principal's office and an errand boy approached us. He asked Father to bring me in. I was eating chocolate, relishing the melodious taste in the core of my heart. But there came a sudden disruption to my joy. I was forced to wrap the chocolate and keep it in its bag before proceeding for the interview. This made me upset; I didn't want to miss the moment of enjoying the taste of chocolate.

I followed orders, and we went into the principal's room. I remember that the principal was wearing white attire; he had a beautiful smile on his face when we entered. He welcomed me and asked a few simple questions like the spelling of "aeroplane", "elephant", etc. Now listen to what I did: I did not utter a word and just looked here and there. I kept my face blank.

Father kept observing me, with the hope that I would answer as he had taught me several times. But my mind was fixed on the chocolate; so, I did not utter a word. The feeling of losing my best friends was also on my mind. The principal kept watching me, hoping to hear the right answer from my mouth. But a deep silence reigned. He waited 10 minutes for me to respond, but lost hope and asked my father to take his child away.

My father with a heavy heart walked out of the room; as expected, his face was red with anger. He asked me why I did not answer the questions, which he had taught me several times. My innocent answer brought a different smile to his face. I didn't know what was going on inside his mind. My answer was, "Why you did not allow me to eat chocolate; because of that, I was sad and angry".

Oh, God what a foolish thing I did. I have a reason for sharing my childhood stories. I want to relate with the power of visualization what I am going to talk about in the next chapter. In fact, I want to set the context so you can walk with me on this journey of visualization. Back to the story: that year I did not get admission to my brother's school. Hearing the news was an exuberant moment for my friends. I felt the same and continued my journey with friends, as usual.

This golden period continued for one year. By this time, I had completed class three in my school happily with my friends. For class four, my father again filled out the form; he was adamant to get me admitted into my brother's school. This time, he left no stones unturned in my preparation for the interview. I had also matured. I did well in the interview. I was successful, and my name was displayed on the school noticeboard for selection to class four. Father was very happy; he immediately took the certificate from my present school.

It was a shock for my friends, but life had to move on. I started a new life in my new school. I found a difference in the syllabus and the way the teachers instructed the students. There were definitely more books to read and more home assignments. Somehow, I felt that things were moving very fast; I was just going with the flow. I was not able to capture the concepts. Everything was moving very fast. School ran from 8 am to 2 pm. I reached home every day at around 3 pm. In the afternoon, I was asked to take a nap for one hour and then study for one hour. I tried to concentrate, but many of the concepts taught in the school were not very clear to me. When I tried to understand, there was a burden in my mind to complete the home assignments.

Somehow, I was not able to gel with the school. On the examinations, I could score marks but not on a par with the few students who earned good marks. I was no longer the blue-eyed boy of the teachers as in the previous school. My confidence went down with each passing day. I started developing the belief of being a mediocre student. I wanted to make a U-turn. What I want to impart is that our belief system is based on the circumstances we pass through. If you view my background, you will note that I was a bright student in my previous school. I would have been a topper. My confidence level would have been very high. My belief would have been as a bright student.

In the new school, gradually over a period of time, my belief shifted from a bright to a mediocre student. Today when I realized this, things look totally different. I have overcome my old belief with a new one, developed in ignorance and based on the circumstances I was going through. Today I am a successful person having scored a very good rank on many examinations at various levels. In my organization, my work is appreciated. I have also received the tag of "best employee".

Going forward and giving you a glimpse of my present life — where technology has made life very easy and this world very small — it is very easy to get connected with school friends; in fact, all our friends are on social media platforms. We communicate at intervals; when I compare their success with mine, I find myself above them. In my organization, I lead a team of one hundred people; it is a dream for many of my friends to reach that cadre. I have all the needed facilities, from a chauffeur-driven car to an expensive flat with all amenities. I live in the financial capital Mumbai.

I have written in my previous book, "Wake Up Your Sleeping Giant" that morning rituals have been a pure transformer of my life. I have been practicing the eight morning rituals every morning for sixty minutes for the last five years, and it has totally transformed me. I can say this with pride. You too can change yourself if you remain committed to your morning habits. If you have not read my previous book, please do read it. It is a game changer.

To conclude this chapter, I would like to say that my belief of being a mediocre student developed because I started accepting the circumstances in front of me. I did not question why I am not able to understand school subjects well. I did not question why I was doing so well in my previous school and what was suddenly happening in the new one. I had the same intelligence; what had changed was only the circumstance. My school had been changed, my friends got changed, and my teachers got changed. The rest was as usual.

Whether my mind did not accept the change, or I did not want to change, I didn't know.

In my subconscious mind, I might not have accepted the new environment. I wanted to go back to my previous school. Life is like this; every one of us has passed through such situations in some way or another. What is required is to accept the truth — the circumstances in which we find ourselves — and see life from a new perspective. The only thing that changes is change". So, embrace it and look for the positivity in it.

Try to explore the new life God has brought to you. Even the cocoon breaks out and becomes a beautiful larva. It struggles to come out and find itself in a new environment — a totally different environment. But with the struggle and the passage of the time, it becomes a beautiful butterfly to be appreciated by everyone. The butterfly becomes a part of nature. It gets totally transformed. The same is true for all of us. If I relate to my school journey, once again, I should have tried to approach my teachers to clear my doubts. I should have taken the pains to reach these teachers during recess and ask them to explain the misunderstood concepts. They would have felt good to see a student come forward like that.

At home, I should have discussed my circumstances with my parents. I could have used their help to make my study concepts clearer. I could have sought out my elder brother for more understanding. I could have practiced more assignments at home and generated questions for the next day to ask my teachers. But instead, I was overwhelmed with the new environment and never asked anything. I simply accepted the circumstances and got pushed back in the race of life. I mentally accepted that I was not able to win against those bright students in the class. This belief was strengthened day by day. I accepted that whatever was happening was truth, and it was my fate.

Now when I look back, I find myself laughing at what I did. Later in upcoming chapters, I will discuss the functions of the mind — specific to the conscious and subconscious mind. You will be shocked to learn the power of the subconscious mind. How your thoughts work and how you attract circumstances in your life will be discussed in detail. I have purposefully narrated my story to make you see that belief is the first seed we plant in our minds; this belief has a limiting character that results in our actions determined by the experiences around us.

In the next chapter, I will cover the belief system. Belief is the foundation of life; and once you are fully able to understand the law of belief, you can take your life to the next level. I have done so in my life. I have had many successes which I will reveal when I get an opportunity to talk to you. Now let's move on and get in-depth knowledge on how a belief system affects our lives.

Happy reading!

Chapter 2

Belief

Imagination is everything. It is the preview of life's coming attractions.

-Albert Einstein

Let me start with a small incident which many of us might have experienced. It's about the moth struggling to come out of the glass window. I was once sitting on a couch in my living room when suddenly I found a moth flying from some distance with full speed; it banged on the glass window. Perhaps the moth wanted to fly into the open sky and couldn't understand the glass window as it was transparent. It felt as if the transparent window could take it to the open sky, but the moth couldn't understand that the window was a trap.

I kept observing the struggle it was making to go out of the window. It was slipping down and would crawl to where it had fallen. Again, it struggle to go out the window. This struggle went for more than half an hour; it slipped and then sat silently on the floor for some time. Again, the same struggle started. From this incident, you see that the moth had a strong belief that the transparent window would take it to the outer world, where it would lead a life of freedom in the open sky. It had a belief that the struggle would lead to that result; but whether the struggle was in the right direction, the moth was not aware of it.

When the moth saw the light and the outer world through the transparent glass window, it felt that it was in the right direction to gain freedom and hence mustered all effort to escape. It had a strong belief system that a continuous struggle could lead to victory; but it was not aware that the struggle of getting out of transparent window was a futile exercise — as it was closed. It had no connection with the outer world. It could come out of its belief system to adopt a change in attitude and hence go free. For this reason, I kept the door on the opposite side of the window open to help it to fly out of the room. With a simple change — trying a different approach — it could have taken a 180-degree switch of direction and found the bright light — the way to open sky on the other side.

In short, the moth could have easily flown out of the room. But the moth could never change its fixed mindset and kept on struggling. What I want you to learn from this small incident is that we humans have also a strong belief system; we do not want to break the chain of deep beliefs seated inside us, which may or may not be true. I want to be more specific about the meaning of the belief to help you to understand clearly. Take the example of a tabletop that rests on four legs. These legs give enough support so it can withstand any pressure of the objects sitting on it. These four legs may be compared to our strong belief systems, and the table top can be compared to our lives — who we are, our personalities, and how we view our lives.

Our lives are based on a belief system we develop. These beliefs go deep down such that all our activities and behaviors stem from the core belief system we gather and develop over a period of time. These beliefs can be right or wrong; whatever we have been seeing in our families and society goes deep inside our subconscious, and we accept it. Over a period of time when we grow as an adult, we should judge this belief system and come out of a fixed mindset if we find that our belief system is in way of progress.

We should aim to grow from a fixed mindset to a growth mindset. In subsequent chapters, I will give enough clarity on the conscious and subconscious minds. Don't worry about these typical words at present. What is more important to note: for success in life, we should have a strong belief guiding the task at hand or the dream life we want to have. Beliefs are like the deep-rooted iron rods pushed into the soil upon which strong buildings are created. They are the base. For anything we want to achieve in life, the first and foremost requirement is to strongly believe in a vision.

We should believe that the activity we want to achieve is a diamond; we will 100% receive the diamond if we work in the right direction and with the right mindset. That strong belief will give the right signal to our brains and trigger a dopamine effect to achieve the goal. Whatever is your dream — it may be buying a big house, getting promotion, becoming healthy, losing weight, generating wealth and more — it is very important to first believe that your dreams can succeed and cannot be negated. You need to have an abundance mindset. You have to believe in yourself first to achieve anything in life.

You must create the right foundation in your brain. This is the first secret to success. Once you have done this and fashioned a strong belief system, you have created the foundation for the other pillars of success, which we will discuss in upcoming chapters. Think of the man who wants to jump from the roof of a high-rise to the roof of an adjacent high-rise. Will the man before jumping think of falling and about what will happen if I he is not able to land on the roof of the adjacent building. If you think deeply and imagine you are in such a situation, what will you think? Definitely before starting your action of jumping, you will gather all the strong points in your mind in order to make the jump a success.

Your mind will be filled with only successful thoughts of achieving the task. You will never bring negative thoughts to your mind at this time. You will develop a strong belief that you will succeed at any cost, and you will land safely on the roof. You will raise your energy level, keep your mind cool, and access where to land safely; and with this thought process, you will have a winning attitude. You will have a strong belief that, yes, you will enjoy success land on the roof of the other building. You will not doubt yourself. This is the crux of success. Belief is everything, and it must be very strong. When you take any task — and if that task is your dream — first you should believe in your heart that you are going to get success.

Many successful people like Bill Gates, Narayan Murthy, Win Oprah, and many more had a dream in their hearts to achieve their visons; they believed in their dreams and took action in the direction of the dream. This helped them achieve their goals. There is a difference between achievement and commitment. In achievement, you are attached to the result. When you achieve success, you are happy from the inside: you are motivated. But when you are not successful, you feel discouraged as you didn't get the result anticipated. You feel weak and leave your assignment midstream. You don't believe in your dreams further, and you feel shattered.

This happens when you are too attached to the result. However, when you are committed, you don't leave the assignment even if you are not successful. Why is this? In your heart, there is a belief that you will attain success, no matter what. Failing is not the outcome. You won't get deterred by small failures. You believe that success is waiting for you; maybe you must try different approaches. Thomas Edison failed 1000 times while developing the light bulb. He never felt discouraged about not reaching success. He was always chasing his dreams and remained committed because he had faith.

He had the belief that he was bound to achieve success. Those thousands of failures were not a discouragement; rather, it was a method of learning. Likewise, when a child starts walking for the first time, it stands and falls several times, but do the parents leave their child? Not at all! Parents remain committed to the child's progress. Parents have faith and share a belief that falling is a part of the journey of learning to walk. One day their child will walk on their own. Both child and parent keep persisting, believing in their actions.

Finally, one day, the child starts walking on two feet. The parents' happiness cannot be compared with any fulfillment in life. This is an example of a strong belief system, where we pursue our dreams until we achieve them. Your goal should be very clear. It can be weight loss, a good job, accumulating wealth, spirituality, and anything you want to. Once you are thorough in your goal setting — and the why is clear — you should believe in that one goal and chase it until you achieve it. Chasing your goal is the mantra for success. In subsequent chapters, I will tell you how to realize your goals with the power of visualization. The foundation of visualization is a strong belief system.

Chapter 3

Thoughts, feelings, and Actions

Logic will get you from A to B.
Imagination will take you everywhere.

-Albert Einstein

In the previous chapter, you learned about the strong belief system that needs to be nurtured, and a strong belief in your dream is one of the pillars of success. Once your belief system is strong and you develop full faith in the dream, you are ready to commit yourself to a set goal. Once your commitment is firm and you are ready to start the journey on the power of faith, you can be rest assured that you are on the right path and will achieve success.

Many people don't achieve success because they are not firm in their commitment and leave the journey in the middle of it. Finishing what you start is the mantra for success; you should remain firm on it. As Earl Nightingale, an American radio speaker and author, has rightly said: success is the progressive realization of a worthy goal. Success is the teacher who wanted to become a teacher, success is the housewife who wanted to be a successful wife, success is the student who wanted to get admitted to a good college, and many more.

If you are moving in the direction of a desired goal, you are successful on your journey. When you are driving from one city to another city, and moving in the right direction, you're on the path to success. You fixed the destination before you started the journey, and then you started driving. You are covering the designated miles to reach the destination. This journey to your destination is the successive realization of your goal — which is your destination. Likewise, in life we must have a goal and must channel our energy to achieve it. This is a journey that you should monitor to see if you are moving in the right direction.

As in the above example, if you take a different route, you will reach a different destination. You will never reach your destination or goal. The same is true with any endeavor in the right direction needed to achieve the dream you have thought about. Recently, I was driving to a destination Lonavala. I realized that when I was driving, I was only driving. You might be thinking what I am talking about; everyone drives when one drives. What I want to say is that when I was driving, my mind was fixed on the road.

I was only thinking about reaching my destination, and my mind was not distracted by other thoughts. I was firm on reaching the destination; using Google maps was my only sole motive at that point of time. I was moving forward, covering the needed miles. My journey to the destination was getting shortened after every mile covered. I want to correlate that similar to achieving your dream destination, you should know how to achieve the current goal and what effort you must put in. Your vision should be very clear: by following a particular strategy, you will achieve success. offer a few examples: for students, it might be studying chapters every day for 7-8 hours with full devotion and the right strategy; for working professionals, it is working smart and completing the priority task; for health-conscious people, it may be losing 15-20 Kg... and so on.

If I relate the example of driving a car, you may observe that you likely had first thought of visiting the destination location and then allowed it to consciously settle in your mind, making a firm decision. Had you not known about the task of driving, would you have thought of driving to another city — maybe 500 miles farther. Obviously not; but since you know about driving, you have the belief that you will achieve the goal of reaching the destination, which is 500 miles away.

This belief is important; with this it, you must venture to try to achieve your dream destination. Driving 500 miles requires courage — the act of moving forward even in fear. Similar to your success journey in any venture you set for yourself, your belief must be very strong, and you need to be courageous. Again, if I can go back to the example of driving: with a strong belief, you started driving the car, but en route to your destination, you face many obstacles like heavy traffic, vehicle breakdown, etc. But after fixing the problem, you continue on.

In nutshell, you applied all means possible to fix the problem to continue on the journey and reach the desired destination. How did this happen? You had faith in yourself and the goal of to reaching the destination. This is life...how life behaves. Challenges and obstacles come when we are on the journey to our destined goal, but we must face the challenges and move forward. You can relate this to any journey like getting your kid admitted to a good school, getting an appointment letter for your dream job, losing your desired weight, venturing into new business, and more.

In all these situations, however small or big, recall how you felt while on your success journey to achieve the desired goal. You will recognize a positive feeling. You were enthusiast about your goal; you always carried a good feeling factor. It is time to learn that positive feelings are very important when on the journey of achieving your goal. If you carry a negative feeling for any reason, you will not be able to reach your destination.

Do you know that feelings and thoughts vibrate at a certain frequency. If your feelings are positive, you attract positive situations and things in life. Likewise, if your feelings are negative, you will attract negative situations and things in life. This is the strange secret of life. As the ocean is filled with water, the earth is surrounded by air; likewise, the mind is surrounded by the sea of mind. All human minds vibrate at different frequencies, based on the feelings and thoughts consumed by the mind. Every now and then, we emit a frequency through our minds into the ether around us; we attract a similar frequency as the one at which our thoughts are vibrating. If our thoughts and feelings are vibrating at a positive frequency, we will attract positive feelings; and if our thoughts and feelings are vibrating at negative frequency, we will attract negative thoughts and circumstances in our life. Just compare the human mind with the radio station we want to tune to in order to listen to our favorite music. To catch the right frequency, we need to tune the radio FM to that frequency. Similarly, we must keep our feelings and thoughts at the right frequency to catch the right frequency of positiveness — which is there in the environment around us.

Why am I telling you these facts? Beliefs, thoughts, and feelings are the foundation of the process of visualization. Later in the chapter, you will learn how visualization becomes a game changer for you. You can learn to create your own destiny with the power of visualization by practicing it daily. The mind is like a fertile land; it does not distinguish between positive thoughts and negative thoughts. What you think, you will become. With the strangest secret, Earl Nightingale clearly displayed that the mind may be compared with a fertile piece of land that does not distinguish between what you are sowing in it. If you sow cotton in the field, you will get a cotton plant; and if you sow a poisonous plant, you will get a poisonous plant.

Likewise, the mind does not care what specific thoughts come pouring in; it will accept any and start working on them. It is our duty to be aware of this and filter the negative thoughts from coming into our minds. We must always tune the frequency of our thoughts from negative to positive if subconsciously we start thinking negative. Our endeavor should be to consciously take positive thoughts into our minds and let a positive feeling build around them. With these positive feelings, we will feel cheerful inside and motivated to march forward.

Once we are in this zone, we should be rest assured that good fortune is going to knock on our doors shortly. The strangest secret is: "You become what you think". If you think about reducing and make the positivity of losing weight the one thought that surround all others, while being cheerful with your daily progress, you are bound to achieve success. Do not bother about the result. Believe in the process and enjoy achieving the desired goal. When you are driving, you should enjoy driving... and the natural beauty on the way to your destination.

Have positive feelings and good thoughts. If you do not enjoy the process, you will miss the enjoyment, which is your right. This is true for other goals; for example, if you want to become wealthy. You should have a positive outlook on what you are doing to become wealthy. Believe in your work and get involved in the process. The process is more important than the result because once you are in process, you will be committed to the task. Ultimately, what counts is action.

Without action, nothing can be achieved. If you gather knowledge but do not implement it, it is just daydreaming. Whatever success has been achieved in this universe is because of massive action taken. Take the case of Thomas Edison again; he failed 1000 times, but he was continuously acting. He took massive action to get success with his persistence. Ideas start in our minds, but then it is our responsibility to implement them.

Take another example: you want to lose weight, say 10 kg in 3 months. To achieve this goal, you might have read many articles or heard from friends and relatives on the topic of weight loss. You might have accumulated enough knowledge to lose weight as you now know every technique. But you will get results only if you implement this knowledge and act. So, implementation and taking massive action is very important. In later chapters, you will learn that you can attract anything in life if you believe it and have positive feelings about it.

Once you have a robust belief in your thoughts and dreams, you need to act in that direction as if you are bound to achieve it. This gives the universe the cue that you are really interested in what you want in life. If you dream of the ideal weight and the body of a Hollywood star, you need to start working on the disciplines required to maintain ideal weight. Discipline may require waking up early in the morning, going for a walk or run, mindful eating and drinking, a good sleeping habit, and maintaining a positive mindset throughout the day. In other words, you must start acting in the direction where you want to go.

If you want to travel around the world, simply dreaming will not help; you need to act and start your journey. It is the same truth for anything we desire in life. If you desire, then you must believe in your dreams. You must remain positive and start taking action so the universe understands your dedication. Once you are in this trajectory, you will get results.

Let me give you one more example. Take the case of an airplane that covers the distance from one city to another; let's say that the total time to cover the two cities is 120 minutes. You might have observed that the flight starts at the right time and reaches its destination city at the right time. On the way, it gets a lot of disturbances — like rough weather and turbulence — but it manages the challenges and lands at the destination on time. It tries to make up for the lost time on account of the turbulence. It never stops but keeps on moving. Similar to life. We must first have a destination fixed in our minds. Without a goal or destination, we will be a flight with no destination, and you are aware of your fate.

All the fuel will be consumed midair and, subsequently, the plane (you) will crash. In a similar fashion, if you do not have a fixed goal, you will be simply moving with the flow of life — wherever life takes you. So, you must have a goal in mind. If you do not, take out a pen and paper and write down your goal in life: what you want to achieve, where you want to see yourself five years down the line, or a long-term vision. It may become a billionaire, buy an expensive home, owning a luxury car, getting a promotion, enjoying a healthy life, etc. Fix your vision, start acting, work toward it, and finally have a safe landing. In subsequent chapters, you will learn how visualization works to achieve your dream goal. You will learn the art of 5 minutes of daily visualization, which will change your life dramatically.

I wish to reiterate that visualization works when you have a solid foundation of feelings, beliefs, thoughts, and actions. In the next chapter, I will lay the foundation of habits, because they are important to maintain consistency in the adventure ahead of you. Once you are used to any activity on a continuous basis, no one can stop you from thriving and achieving your goal. I want you to develop the habit of practicing visualization daily to start attracting your dream life.

Chapter 4

Building Habits

What you think you become. What you feel, you attract. What you imagine, you create.

-Buddha

A habit is a crucial part of life; without it, consistency is unattainable, and consistency is eminent in reaching our success goals. We might have beautiful desires in life: to become rich and famous personalities, for example, in the end, we cannot catch our dreams if we feel it's impossible and what is presently going on is accepted as our fate. But this is not true. We can become billionaires, popular singers, popular Rockstars, even the CEO of a billionaire company, or the best motivational speaker. We undermine ourselves when we think that those personalities are different, and we are not even one per cent close to their level. This belief subdues us, and we remain slaves to poor thoughts.

We cannot grow with such thoughts; we find ourselves adjusting to our present lives or accepting that whatever is happening to us is our fate. Fate has been predetermined, and we cannot do anything about it. We start settling for less and go with the flow. In this regard, a study shows that we are what we think. Author Anthony Robbins very well enumerates in his book, "Awaken the Giant Inside," that the power of decision can change our lives, the moment we decide on something. It is as simple as making a decision, and we immediately take a U-turn. We start seeing a change because of a small firm decision we had been procrastinating on doing.

If you refer to dictionary, you will find the word "decision", meaning to cut oneself off from ideas holding us back and taking a different path altogether given what we think is right and appropriate. We all know what is right or wrong, but the human tendency is to always find a path to our comfort zone and finally settle in it. Our comfort zones make us feel satiated and inhibit us from acting or taking any strain in life. This leads to complacency, and we lose the inborn talent hidden within us.

We only need to look at other people's status, witness their success, see how rich they are, and then make our minds understand that those successful people were born with a silver spoon, with God's blessing. We highly regard those people, and they become our ideal. We mentally scuttle their good fortune such that becoming an ideal personality is not our cup of tea. If we look at the history of rich entrepreneurs like Ambani, Tata etc., we will find that everyone had struggled initially; nobody was born rich.

They were born with the same physical and mental capabilities as us; but one thing that has made the difference is their mindsets. They had that rigid mindset of discipline and punctuality, which made all the difference based on the decisions they made. My question is: if people who start from scratch can become billionaires, why can't you? Think about it. **All power is within you; you can do anything and everything.**" These are the lines of Swami Vivekananda. I have full faith in this one statement of his; I have experienced it. Like a common person, I used to be in my comfort zone, watching TV late at night and waking up late in the morning only to rush to the office. Nothing was bright for me because I was going with the flow of the office pressure. This is true for students and personalities in different professions who wake up late in the morning and rushing off to school, the office, or to do business.

A lot of people have the habit of checking their emails and WhatsApp messages first thing in the morning. This is unnecessary as you get entangled. You lose control of yourself, and your life is directed by others. You lose the kick of the day. The day you should have owned it is now being controlled by someone else. Have you ever analyzed why this is happening?

The answer is not following a morning routine once you wake up. Your morning hour after your wake up is your victory hour. You need to grab that one hour after you wake up to charge yourself for the entire day. Once you do the morning rituals taught in "Grab Your Victory Hour", you will be at the top of your energy level for the entire day — and feel the difference from day one. "Now" is when you must change yourself. While reading this book, you are getting a hint in your subconscious to change yourself. Please follow your inner conscience and hear your inner voice.

It is a one-moment decision to decide to change yourself. There is no other way. Once you have decided that you need to improve your habits, you must remain firm. I am telling you that you will become a changed person when you decide to change your habits and adopt a good one. Habit requires discipline and consistency. It is quite human to fall back into your comfort zone when you adopt a good habit. You may be consistent for a few days, but there is every chance that you will return to square one in time.

However, there is a way to come out of it: be consistent in your mindset of maintaining discipline. Research tells us that anything we practice for 21 days will become a habit, and then after 21 days, we cannot live without those good habits. I have experimented on myself; if I am unable to perform my morning ritual, I feel a void in my life. Wherever I am, I religiously perform it. I wake up at 5.00 am every day; when the alarm clock rings, I immediately walk to the clock — as I keep it at a distance — dismiss it and then start my morning ritual.

I purposely keep the alarm clock at a distance to break my sleep pattern. As noted, it's a human tendency to go back to your comfort zone. I remember my first day of a morning ritual. I was excited to wake up in the morning, but my motivation was a little less on the second day. There was a feeling inside my mind that I had not slept enough and should sleep for one more hour. It is effortless to become trapped in the habits we have been following for ages; we live in inertia for change. We are very satisfied with our lifestyles. If we ponder what is holding us back, we will find that we don't want to shift out of our comfort zones. The inertia of rest is holding us back. Newton's law of motion states that a body will remain in the state of rest until and unless an external force is applied on it.

This is true for the human body; our comfort zone is our inertia of rest, and our decision to change comes from a force within that compels us to move into a more uncomfortable zone. If you are determined to change the habit of waking up early in the morning, you will immediately change to a different personality at that very moment of making the decision.

As noted earlier, any habit performed continuously for 21 days becomes a part of life; and after 21 days, we enjoy the new habit. When we miss the habit for a day, we get an inner call that we are lacking something in our daily routine, and we do not feel 100% for the entire day. The first seven days of getting into the good habit are crucial; in this period, we have every chance to fall back on the previous comfort zone from where we had started the journey.

Not to fall back, you need to have the strong mindset of maintaining the consistency of getting into the new habit zone. You must keep yourself calm and believe that you are improving every day by 1%, even though these changes will not be very visible to you initially.

In the book, "Compound effect", the author says that little changes every day will have a compound effect This is true. Do not fall prey to your mind renouncing the new habit being developed. The mind has the habit of dragging us into our comfort zone. If you can control your mind for the initial seven days, I assure you that you have won the race. This is a difficult period to pass through; it is a known fact that there is every chance for you to slide back to your original place of the journey from *where you started but do not do that. Become conscious of these facts and win over your* mindset.

In the next seven days, from the 8th to the 14th day, you will find improvement building in yourself. You will feel good, and your conscience will tell you that you are becoming a changed person. Here also, a positive feeling of change has come to you; but there is every chance of falling back into your original comfort zone. The simple rule of thumb is not to follow your mind. Follow your intelligence, which is above the mind. The mind has the habit of disrupting you, but your intelligence protects you from negative thoughts.

Maintain the consistency of the new habit for 14 days. Do not miss a single day; slowly, you will reach your semi-goal post of 14 days journey. Yes, when you have completed your 14 days — I would say, based on my experience — that you have acquired 90% of the good habit, and now you are a changed person. People will start looking at you differently, and you will feel proud of your achievement and your decision to transform yourself internally.

Next is the journey from Day 15 to Day 21. This is the honeymoon period, where you will find that you cannot live without performing those habits. An internal call will be pushing you to perform those habits. This is the period of urgency, where you cannot live a single day without the good habits you have developed. I can vouch that after this 21 day journey, you will be a changed and transformed person. You will have a different personality altogether.

This 21-day activity is the game changer for your life, which is true for any habit you want to develop. Further in subsequent chapters, I help you build on this 21-day habit. The secret is based on a platform called, "habit". Your daily visualization for 5 minutes is based on habit formation. Maintain it for 21 days, and you will be a winner.

Chapter 5

What is Visualization

See yourself living in abundance and you will attract it.

-Rhonda Byrne

Visualization is an ancient technique practiced by many successful people in the universe. This technique is part of your morning routine because practicing helps you to become the person of your dreams. Your dream can be turned into reality. It is also called the law of attraction. You attract dreams inspired by your thoughts. I will tell you in detail how to practice this technique.

You will slowly realize that the universe is bringing the things you have wanted into your life. Opportunities start coming, and you start taking benefits from them. You become part of those opportunities and immediately start acknowledging their worth. You have been waiting for this miracle to happen for years; and suddenly, situations start moving in your favor. Visualization always works and has worked for thousands of people.

In 1954, Roger Bannister, a noted athlete, decided to run 1 mile in 4 minutes. He was told that this was impossible. Roger Bannister did not believe in other people's mindsets. Also, the town's physicians said it was humanly impossible to run 1 mile in 4 minutes. Bannister was determined to break the long-held myth. He started visualizing the entire event of running and started practicing every day.

He visualized his victory every day and clearly heard the clapping sounds of his victory from the audience. He saw the entire event of victory in his mind; not once but several times. When D-day came, it was to the surprise of everyone that he broke the record and ran 1 mile in less than 4 minutes. After that, many athletes broke the record of running 1 mile in less than 4 minutes. This is the power of visualization.

Scientific studies have proven that mental training with visualization is an effective strategy for many forms of athletics, from throwing darts and basketball to sprinting and weight training, to Olympic competitions. Olympic athletes from various disciplines, including gymnastics, diving, judo, and fencing use visualization to prepare for competition.

In "Awaken the Giant Inside", Tony Robbins gives the example of Mike Tyson. Tyson wanted to become the best boxer in the world and accoladed as number one. He followed the principle of visualization. Every day, he visualized that he was the best boxer in the world. He was getting victory after victory, winning medals. He clearly saw that he was crushing his opponents and was declared champion. Today, we witness Mike Tyson as the champion in boxing. His dream turned into reality. Many successful people have realized the power of visualization. They started practicing visualization in their daily work. Slowly, they found that things began working as expected, and they became successful day by day.

 At this point, you might be inquisitive to know how visualization works and how you can follow the steps of visualization to experiment on yourself and become the person of your choice to improve your life. Everyone wants to improve and achieve success, whatever phase of life they are in. We often try to achieve our dream but later feel that these dreams are not achievable. We compromise with the weak thoughts coming into our minds, and then we settle for less. We become victims of the Imposter Syndrome.

Research explains, "Imposter Syndrome is the condition of feeling anxious and not experiencing success internally, despite being high performing in external, objective ways. This condition often results in people doubting their abilities". This happens to everyone; as a result, we get satiated by the flow of life and don't adventure to achieve our dreams.

I have read many articles on visualization and wanted to test the technique by following the steps indicated. I practiced and found to my utter surprise that the goal I had dreamed of started coming to me as an opportunity. I believe it to be a ladder for success and achieving my dream. I started every day, visualizing, and writing a book on motivation. I sought to help my readers improve their lives. Today the result is in front of you —you are reading this book.

Yes, it works. This book is my fourth in the Morning Series. Visualization is one of my daily routine rituals, and I have followed it arduously daily. As a reader, you might have varied dreams' some of you want to become a successful professional, a successful CEO, a good homemaker, a motivational speaker, a best-seller author, etc., and the list continues. Visualization can bring about change and help you achieve your goals.

Whatever goal you have in your mind, the thought of making that goal come true should always be at the top of mind. For proper visualization, you must devote 5 minutes to the morning ritual hour. The goal you want to achieve should be visible as if you have already achieved it. Let's say you want to be successful in an interview to get promoted in the organization you work for. You need to visualize the process. Visualize reading many articles about the questions to be asked in the interview. Visualize the day before your interview that you are fully prepared and enjoy a peaceful sleep the night before.

The next morning, you are getting ready for the interview. Your attire is well arranged with coordinating colors of your shirt, trousers, tie, blazer, etc. You must feel the entire process as if it is happening to you. You see yourself traveling on interview day and sitting in the waiting room with other candidates. Feel the confidence on your face. See the last candidate coming out of the interview room; then your turn comes next. Visualize clearly how you are knocking on the door and sitting in chair. See the panel members, hear the questions each member asks, and how confidently you are answering them with a smile on your face. See clearly that all the interview members are happy with your knowledge; in fact, everyone is impressed.

The interview members feel satisfied as if you are the candidate they are looking for. See clearly that they are saying "best of luck". With humbleness, you thank them and come out of the interview room. You feel the joy on your face and finally visualize that you got selected for the interview and have an offer in hand.

This is one of the examples I give to help you understand the concept of visualization. The same mental journey can be for any dream you want to achieve. Thoughts in a positive direction are bound to attract positiveness and afford you success. The crux of the matter is that you must experience the feeling of success on your visualization journey and see the end result you want.

Visualization has the power to make you familiar with the situation you are about to encounter. You can apply this technique to any activity. Suppose you have to give a presentation to your boss or a client; you can visualize the entire proceedings in your mind. You can see everyone in the conference room giving you a thumbs-up for a wonderful presentation.

Practice it and you will feel fulfilled, even before you grab success. It will feel like you are encountering a real situation. The actual event to occur will be your second victory. The first victory was already won in your mind. From today onward, set aside five minutes for the visualization process. This is one of the morning rituals in your victory hour. Practice it daily, and you will see the difference in your life. You find yourself ahead on the journey of becoming an extraordinary person.

Chapter 6

How Visualization Works

Whatever you hold in your mind on a consistent basis is exactly what you will experience in your life.

-Tony Robbins

We all have read that matter can neither be created nor destroyed. It simply transforms from one form to another. Also, matter in physics is defined as energy. All human beings are made up of matter and hence we all are energy. All living and nonliving things in this universe are matter and energy. At the core level is only one energy, and that energy is distributed and flows through all of us — whether a living or a nonliving being.

When there is energy, there will be a frequency; hence all matter in this universe is vibrating at a certain frequency.

Our feelings, thoughts, beliefs, and actions have a frequency; at any point in time, we are vibrating at a particular one. A frequency has the unique character of attracting a similar frequency. If the frequency is positive, it will attract positive situations or people in our lives. Likewise, if a frequency is negative, it will attract negative situations or people. To further make the concept of energy and its frequency clear, take the example of electricity. Electricity in the universe is the same throughout. The same electricity runs the fan, refrigerator, microwave, air conditioner, and any other electrical item. The function of the equipment is different, but the underlying energy of their performance is electricity.

Hence all equipment is interconnected through the function of electricity and performs their activities as per the functionalities built in, taking leverage of electricity. Likewise, all humans are connected with a common thread of energy, i.e., we all are performing our daily tasks, based on the energy we possess. Every single moment, we are vibrating at a certain frequency and, accordingly, attracting situations or people into our lives. This is the basic tenet of the law of attraction, and visualization works on this principle.

You may ask, how to attract your goals and achieve what you ever wanted in life. Learn the science behind it, and you will be amazed. As noted, all living and nonliving things in this universe are energy and hence vibrate at a certain frequency. I divide frequency into two types: positive frequency and negative frequency. Frequencies have the characteristics of attracting similar frequency. Positive frequency will attract positive frequency, and negative frequency will attract negative frequency.

If you think positive, you will attract positive circumstances in your life; and if you think negative, you will attract negative circumstances. Relate the concept of frequency to the radio station you want to tune to. If you want to listen to your favorite radio station, you must adjust the frequency of that radio station; then you are aligned to enjoy your favorite songs. Likewise, your thoughts have a frequency; to attract the dreams of your choice, you must tune your mind to positive thoughts. You must ensure that you vibrate at a positive frequency. As stated, even nonliving things are energy, vibrating at a certain frequency. Here is the secret: your goals and dreams are vibrating a certain frequency; to attract that goal, your mind should also vibrate at the equivalent frequency.

Let me make it simpler with an example. Suppose you want to purchase a dream apartment as your goal. It is a matter of energy; hence it is vibrating at a certain frequency. To have that dream in your possession, you must match the frequency of your apartment, which means you have to think that you are in possession of it.

Let us delve a bit deeper. To achieve your dream, your thoughts should align with the frequency of the apartment; it is possible only when you tune your mind to the right frequency and start believing that the apartment is yours. You feel good about the possession. Soak up feeling of fulfillment. Bring a genuine smile to your face for this victory. This is the deep secret of visualization. Practice this exercise with a belief until you achieve your dream. Have deep faith in the power of visualization and practice it daily without fail. It just requires 5 minutes.

Chapter 7

The Power of Visualization

*Your life is a reflection of your thoughts.
Think well.*

-Danielle Pierre

You have learned the power of habits and why they are the pillars upon which success resides. For any good habit to be formed, you need consistency; and consistency requires effort and stubbornness to achieve your goal. If you are not stubborn and rigid, you cannot develop habits. Your goal should always be in front of you; you should day in and day out think of that goal. The goal should not let you sleep. It should be your" One Thing."

I am relating the power of habits in a morning routine because I want you to have consistency in performing visualization every day for 5 minutes. You need to be consistent. Your goal is your vision and the goal you want to achieve should be in your visualization exercise. You might have read and experienced that a magnifying glass, when placed on a piece of paper under a bright sun, burns the paper.

Similarly, when you visualize your goal everyday with full concentration, you will hit your goal and achieve whatever you want in life. I have personally experienced the power of visualization and have been practicing it for the last five years. I want to relate my goal of becoming an author of non-fiction books as an example. I visualized every day that I was writing a book and my books were getting published.

Today, I am the author of four books and continuing my journey. As I write these lines, I have the goal of becoming a world-renowned motivational speaker, travelling the world and telling people about good morning habits. I am on a journey of achieving my dream just as I am practicing visualization every day for its outcome. You may be curious how visualization works and how by simple doing it, one can achieve the dream of one's choice.

Well, I had the same doubts and inquisitiveness when I heard about visualization. I started researching visualization and was really impressed to know the science behind it. I wanted to practice the power of visualization on myself. I was determined to share my experience with the universe. It was a marvelous experience that has now become a part of my everyday morning ritual. Now revealing the research behind the power of visualization, hold your breath and read patiently what I am going to tell you in the next lines. Assimilate the facts as they are and surrender your thoughts what is coming forth.

Let us understand the science behind the success of achieving your goal through visualization. Research has found that the brain has two spheres: one is the conscious mind, and the other is the subconscious mind. I promised earlier in this book that I would tell you in detail about the subconscious mind. Now the journey begins. The conscious mind is the reasoning mind. Whatever you see around and feel around you is because of your conscious mind. It analyses the situations around you and makes decisions on how to feel about them. For example, if you travel to see the beauty of nature and appreciate it, it is because of your conscious mind. On the other hand, your subconscious mind is subjective and does not question anything.

It takes things and situations as your conscious mind perceives them. The subconscious mind simply acts, based on the direction of the conscious mind. If you feel that the circumstances you are in at present are not good, your subconscious mind gets the message and starts behaving negatively. It brings a negative reaction to you, and you start feeling negative or fear starts crippling you. You become anxious and negative feelings overpower you.

Similarly, if your conscious mind perceives a situation as positive, then a positive message goes to your subconscious mind. You start feeling positive and attract positive situations in your life. The conscious mind is like the captain of the ship who sees the sea far off in the direction of the voyage, looking for the obstacles if any. The captain gives orders to his crew inside the ship, and they take command. The crew members are not able to see the water surface.

The crew's job is only to take command and act. They turn the direction of the ship as per the command from the captain. They simply navigate the ship. Our subconscious mind is like the crew. The subconscious mind takes the command from the conscious mind and acts accordingly to specific commands of the conscious mind. It doesn't have the power of reasoning. It simply accepts the command and doesn't judge whether the command is true or not. It acts on the command.

This is the biggest secret of the mind. I was amazed to read the research; when I went deep into my own research, I found that many successful people know of this power of subconscious mind. They have leveraged the power of mind. They knew how the mind functions and utilized the concept to their advantage.

The subconscious mind is like fertile land. As a piece of land is always ready to grow any seed— whether a good or a poisonous crop — it doesn't question it. It simply takes the seed and over a period, brings the result. It is like our attitudes toward life and the thoughts associated with them. We implant our thoughts in our mind. If we plant good thoughts in our mind, good situation will come in our life; likewise, if we plant evil thoughts in our mind, then we will face evil circumstances in life.

The subconscious mind doesn't question; it takes these thoughts as it is from the conscious mind. The biggest question is: can we consciously give suggestions to our subconscious mind. Can we make our subconscious believe and act according to our dreams. Yes, research says that we can give suggestions to our subconscious mind and make it work in our favor. How is this possible?

You might now have a lot of question about harnessing your subconscious to your advantage. Well, here comes the power of visualization. Your subconscious mind does not question, as noted. It simply takes command of the conscious mind and, accordingly, bring situations in our lives. Have your ever experienced remembering a close relative or friends, and within a few minutes, you get a call from that person?

Yes, this is an experience of the subconscious mind. Your conscious mind thought of the person; your subconscious mind took it as a command and brought in front of you that very same person. The subconscious brings experience based on conscious thoughts. Now I will reveal how you can achieve your dream by leveraging the power of subconscious mind. Listen carefully to what I am going to tell you. For your goal to come true, you need to visualize in your mind that you have already achieved your goal.

For example, if you want to be billionaire, living a life of freedom, you must clearly visualize that you have $1 billion in your bank account. You have to clearly see the amount as the credit balance. Your mind should accept this fact and develop a strong belief in it. You must visualize and think that the event has already occurred; with that, positive thoughts and feeling are coming into your mind. When you consciously see $1 billion in your bank account, your subconscious mind does not question it and takes the associated feelings and thoughts associated—as it is.

The role of the subconscious mind is to bring to you an experience associated with your thoughts. You had implanted the thought of $1 billion in your bank account, so your subconscious mind will now endeavor to bring situations to you that make you see in the physical $1 billion over a period of time. Your mind will be tuned to the action, which will bring the desired outcome. This is the power of visualization.

Similarly, you can have any number of goals in life; it may be reducing your weight and becoming healthy, enjoying career development, becoming a good housemaker, and more. Visualization works for everyone and every good idea you think about. The power of visualization can be harnessed once it is practiced daily. That is why I have stressed practicing visualization every day for 5 minutes. You should be consistent in your habit for it to work.

By consistently working on visualization every morning for 5 minutes, you will be implanting the seeds of your dream in your subconscious mind; it then starts believing it and brings the experiences associated with visualization. Remember that you must clearly see the goal you want to achieve. You must see that the goal for which you are aiming, you have already achieved.

When you visualize the goal, you have already achieved, bring a feeling of achievement of your goal in your mind— a feeling of positiveness and fulfillment of achieving your goal. You must feel in your mind that how your friends, immediate family, and relatives will react when they see your success. These thoughts and feeling should be a part of your visualization exercise. Once you

practice it, you are bound to get results and
achieve your dream goal.

Chapter 8

How to Practice Visualization

Let a person radically alter his thoughts, and he will be astonished at the rapid transformation it will affect in the material conditions of his life.

-Napolean Hill

Up to now, you have learned the facts behind visualization and how it works. Now, you will learn how to practice visualization and make it a daily morning habit. Remember that during the visualization process, your goal should deeply sink into your mind; the most important principle here is to believe that your subconscious will work as per your suggestions. So, let's begin and learn to harness the power of visualization.

I have always recommended utilizing the morning hours for practicing visualization as these hours are the best time to sink deep thoughts into your subconscious mind. First and foremost, assign 5 minutes to the activity as your morning ritual. Please read my book, Grab your Victory Hour, to learn the 8 principles of morning rituals. One of the principles I talk about is practicing visualization every day for 5 minutes. Undertake the following steps:

1. Find a comfortable place in your home, preferably a corner of a room, where there is no disturbance.
2. Sit comfortably, either by crossing your legs on the floor or you can sit up straight on chair.
3. Relax and take a deep breath. Feel a perfect calmness in your mind and that your body is totally relaxed.
4. If thoughts are coming into your mind, let them come, accept them, and let them go. Imagine your thoughts as clouds appearing and

moving. The idea is not to get attracted to your thoughts.

5. Once you are relaxed mentally and physically, close your eyes and feel a perfect silence within you. Take a deep breath in and breathe out. Once again, take a deep breath and breathe out. Yes, you now have set the perfect ground to plant the seed of your visualization.

6. With your eyes closed, think about the goal you want to achieve. Bring that goal in front of you and feel that you have achieved your goal.

7. In the process of feeling you have achieved your goal, you will see the entire process of success in your mind, taking the time to receive congratulations from your friends and relatives. It is important to see the outcome you want. You must see your goal achieved.

I will now offer examples that relate to your success journey and the goal you want to achieve. The same example from the previous chapter was a job promotion. You must visualize that you are preparing for the interview, accumulating all requisite knowledge, and appearing for the interview. All panel members are very happy with your answers. You are enjoying the process and finally you are selected. During the entire visualization process, you must feel that the picture you are creating in your mind is real; your actual feelings of joy and success should follow. Think for moment that you have received the promotion letter and how you feel once you know that you have been promoted to higher level. Bring about the same joy in your visualization as if you have already achieved.

As mentioned, the subconscious mind will never question what is coming from the conscious mind. You are consciously creating a real picture; and the same is getting absorbed in your subconscious mind. The role of the subconscious is to bring the event true to what your conscious mind is seeing. This is the power of the subconscious mind.

Similarly, you can visualize your ideal weight, accumulating wealth, having a happy life, accumulating great health, and more. Remember that your subconscious mind has infinite intelligence; but the problem is that it does not know that it knows. It has the answer for everything. I urge you to harness the power of your subconscious and use it for your benefit through the power of visualization. May I repeat Swami Vivekananda: " You have all power within you , you can do anything and everything".

Finally, and before concluding this chapter, I advise you not to limit yourself. As you practice visualization, you will find the power of your subconscious mind unfolding. From today going forward, start your journey. The best time for practicing visualization is during morning hours after you wake up when your mind is in a pure state. However, you can practice it at any time when you are calm within. I suggest finding a secluded place where no one will disturb you for 5 minutes.

Good luck in embarking on a new journey.

Chapter 9

Conclusion

To accomplish great things we must first dream, then visualize, then plan.... believe.... act!

-Alfred A. Montapert

I hope that the idea of visualization is clear and now you will embark on the journey and reap the benefits. I am on a mission to help people realize their dreams seamlessly. To conclude, I would like to give the example of Michael Phelps, the world-record holder of multiple Olympic gold medals in swimming, and as how he leverages visualization before each race. In an interview, he recounts seeing himself swimming the perfect race in his mind, and then he does it in a real life. This has been one of the biggest reasons for achieving such amazing results.

I recall Tony Robbins telling a story about an experiment conducted with three groups of basketball players. One group was told to practice throwing from the free throw line a certain number of times every day for six weeks. One group was told not to practice at all. The last group was told to practice only in their minds, but to make sure they visualized themselves making the perfect short every time. After six weeks, the researcher tested all three groups to see which had made the most baskets. You can probably guess the results. The third group, the one that had only practiced in their minds, made more shots than either of the other two groups.

I am sure that with the above two real examples, you can very well understand the power of visualization. Now make visualization your daily habit and practice it diligently for 5 minutes. You will experience the difference. Please let me know about your experience at gyansnarayan22@gmail.com.

Looking forward to hear from you. All the best!

Glimpse of my published book in the series- "Wake Up Your Sleeping Giant"

Scan QR code to Grab your copy

Because of the umpteen pressure in today's hectic lifestyle, we all are in the whirlpool of just leading the life where life is taking us. At this juncture, you as a professional will be in a sales job, marketing job, administrative job, MNC executive, Corporate CEO etc. You are doing what is necessary, but you cannot find the time for yourself which you want, but somehow life comes in between, and you have to drop the idea which you think can change your well-being as well. You are not alone in this universe facing such an issue of balancing life and work. Many professionals are facing this issue. This is the problem statement, and the generations are passing through this problem. You are facing this problem, but you feel helpless to change your life and lifestyle and give time to your family. Don't you? This book will try to solve all your problems, and you will be a changed personality after reading this book. You will discover in this book a hidden giant sleeping inside you, just waiting for your direction to activate and do wonders for you. You have infinite potential which you are not aware of. This will be revealed to you in the later chapters. Everyone in this universe has problems, whether he is a company CEO, a multi-billionaire, a working professional, or any human being. Yes, the problem exists with everyone, but he is successful and knows how to cope with the problem. How to come victorious of that problem. Does this require a mindset change? Whether you have a fixed mindset or a growth mindset? You don't know, but while reading through the chapters, you will get to know the truth behind the different mindsets and how you can cultivate a growth mindset which can give a different lens of the problem you are going through. Are you a professional who is aspiring for promotion in your job? Are you a professional who wants to have more energy to guide your team? Are you a professional who cannot meet the sales target and wants to meet the target? Are you a professional who wants to climb up the corporate ladder much faster than your colleagues? As a top management professional of your organization, are you lacking the energy to convince for joint ventures? The problems are many, but in essence, these are not the problems but the lack of tightening of the nuts and bolts of the brain. Yes, what I am claiming is true! These are not all the problems, but the result of the fixed mindset, which to date you have not changed but nothing to worry about as now you are in the right hand. Your book in your hand will mentor you to change yourself and bring all success you deserve. The principles talked about in the book will bring you laurels in your life. After reading this book, you will be a changed personality. You will change completely, and good fortunes will come to you. Many a time, we feel that we don't have time. But is it so? Then why are so many successful personalities in any field you take? I will not name them which you know better, but have you ever thought why they are successful and Billionaire? It's not that they have more than 24 hours in a day. They are also equally capable like you, but they are different today. Why? There must be some secrets they are following that you are unaware of. I will walk you through all those secrets which a successful person follows. There is one formula: "If anyone can do it successfully, you too can do it". Success always leaves clues, and you need to follow those clues to become the same successful person. As I will reveal in the chapters, you have infinite potential, and only a spark is needed to ignite that sleeping giant within yourself. I will reveal all the clues of the successful people which will make you another successful personality that the world will discuss. Then it will become your moral responsibility to propagate the wisdom you will read in this book. There is a Burning Desire within you to do something different; therefore, you are reading this book, and I can vouch that this first step of yours will lead you to cross the bridge, leading to good fortune. Research shows that (FBC)- faith, burning desire, and consistency- will move the mountains. Roger Bannister, an athlete with a clear vision of becoming the best runner in the world by setting a record of running one mile in under four minutes, had faith in his vision. He continuously dreamt of running one mile in less than four minutes. This was humanly impossible, and many doctors in the town said it was impossible for a human being to run 1 mile in 4 minutes. But it was the sheer determination of Roger Bannister to create the record. He dreamt of his victory; he practiced intensely. Every day he woke up at 4 am and practiced. In his mind, there was no other thought but to win the milestone. The entire Universe is the witness to what happened on May 6th, 1954. Roger Bannister broke the world record, and to the surprise of all the doctors in the town, he achieved the record of running 1 mile in 3 minutes and 54 seconds. How was this possible? Was it something unnatural? Was it something extraordinary? Yes, Roger Bannister's determination to succeed was the first stepping stone to his success. He believed in his belief to stand victorious and achieve the world record. He developed a burning desire to achieve the milestone he had seen in his mind, and his consistency in practice daily brought laurels to him. He got many accolades. The entire Universe congratulated him. Some even told him that he was lucky. But the harsh reality only Roger knows. His success was not a single-day success but a consistent and persistent effort. It was his dedicated and consistent effort to wake up every morning at 4 am and start practicing. Think about the same situation in your life. You are also like Roger Banister in your field. You can achieve anything in your career if you are determined to achieve that. Today as a working professional, you might have targets to meet, and you find it difficult and uncomfortable to attend presentations for business review. You are being questioned about the business gap. You have only answered, "Definitely, in the coming quarter or the next month, you will achieve the target". But again, the same situation arises. In the next business review meeting, you face the same situation of the percentage gap in the business figures you were supposed to meet, and you have also committed to achieving that. Still, you were not able to achieve it. Whereas some of your colleagues can achieve the target and get good remarks from the top management in the review meeting. What makes the difference between you and him? For example, if you are a sales professional, you may say that your counterpart's territory has more potential, his products are more demanding in that territory and so on. Similar is true for the Head of the Corporate Verticals. Some Vertical Heads can attract good reviews in the business conference meeting, whereas others get direction to improve further. Why does this happen? When teams are aligned for the vertical heads to assist him in his job, why is one vertical head always a blue-eyed boy of the top management and others are not? There must be some game-changer rules which the other person is following and that you are not following. But don't worry. This book is deep research of the successful person's various activities, which the author has vetted. Yes, the practices in this book have been experimented by me, and I have found a sea change in my personality and well-being. I am continuing the journey and assure you that if you follow and practice the principles in the book, you will be a changed personality with many successful vibes. **You will realize the hidden potential within you which was sleeping till now,** and I call this hidden potential your **"SLEEPING GIANT".** This book has been written with a lot of masterpieces and research work. It is the second in the series of the earlier book published by the author, "Grab your Victory Hour", which has been widely appreciated by readers for bringing a change in their life and personality.

The first chapter of this book, "Wake up your Sleeping Giant", talks about the "The Power of Morning Hour", where you will realize how beautiful is the morning hours and how you have missed all these days not utilizing the benefit of those golden hours which can set the tone of the day for you.

The second chapter talks about "Setting the stage for success and preparing you for the morning routine", as facts will be revealed to you about how to utilize the morning hour and make yourself ready for the aggressive fight for the day and which in turn will make you look aggressive in your work. You will progress much faster in your professional career.

The third Chapter talks about "Mindset Matters: How you start your day with a positive attitude" and gives insights into eight morning rituals that will completely transform you. It guarantees you mental and physical energy, which will help you take complete charge of the day. You will rise on the Corporate Ladder with the mental energy you generate.

The fourth chapter discusses "Productivity Hacks: Maximizing your time and efficiency" and reveals the secret to maximizing your time and efficiency in your work. You will learn how efficiently you can concentrate on your work, which will give you immense satisfaction.

The Fifth Chapter talks about "Planning and Prioritization: Organizing your tasks and goals" and how these two Ps are essential to achieving victory in your life and achieving any target, whether be Sales, Marketing, administrative skills, business ventures etc. In this chapter, you will learn about the application of important principles in your work, which will make a much difference in the style of functioning you have been following till now.

This book promises to awaken the sleeping giant within you and bring you a changed personality with loads of success and good fortunes. This book is for working professionals who want to streamline their work at the office, want to make progress in their career, and quickly climb up the corporate ladder.

Glimpse of my maiden book in the series- "Grab Your Victory Hour"

Scan QR code to Grab your copy.

The sweetest and most joyful period of a lifetime is childhood. Reminiscing on my childhood days with my elder brother who was two years older than me, we were forced to wake up at 4:30 A.M to memorize the subjects taught in the school. My father used an antique alarm clock to wake both of us up. At that time, we were in preschool. Gradually we grew with this morning routine of waking up early. As time went by, our college days began and now we are both working professionals. My elder brother is currently not a morning person, but I have maintained the habit of waking up in the morning. I appreciate the habit of waking up early imbibed in me.

Every parent desire to make their kids shine and get the best results in class and above that, rank first place in school. At that time, I found that I was forced to wake up, but then there was no clarity in my mind about what I was reading and what was getting inside my head. Instead, I would feel sleepy and maybe after a lapse of 45 minutes, my brain and mind would open and I could now read the chapters.

Some research says that morning is the best time for cramming and my father agreed with this. However, I also found that this sentence also has another meaning for my father. My father made doubly sure that we had not slept back and that we were busy reading the books. The sound of our cramming might have given him a sense of fulfilment that kids are learning and their morning hours are best utilized. My brother and I kept on realizing that we were only gainfully utilizing only one of the two hours from 4.30 A.M. to 6.30 A.M. for study, but we dare not say this to our father as he was a strict disciplinarian. This concept of waking up early in the morning led me to research on utilizing the morning's best waking hours. Everyone desires to dream big and achieve their goals like wealth, peak of their career, wisdom, etc. And so was my dream. But the question is how many of us can connect and achieve the goal of our choice? We all have immense potential to achieve whatever we want in life.

In Swami Vivekananda's words, human souls have infinite potential and can achieve anything. This statement is true but requires wings and a burning desire to achieve what we need to accomplish in life. I have come across many people in my life who were students, professionals, and teachers. I observed that every personality I have interacted with has its routines. Some studying late at night and some waking up early in the morning but then they feel sleepy and inactive the entire day. They were missing the day's power pack. They want to change their habits but somehow, they can't. After much of my research on morning waking habits, listening to many podcasts, and reading several books, I concluded that the best way to utilize the morning after waking is first to CHARGE ONESELF WITH A SEQUENCE OF MORNING RITUALS. These morning rituals takes about 60 minutes, and I call this time "Victory Hour".

I have experimented with a series of morning rituals to energize me for the entire day and give me a new outlook for my journey towards becoming an extraordinary person. With my deep learning of morning habits, I desire to write about the morning rituals so that my readers can claim their 'victory hour' and utilize the hour as the best way to charge themselves for the entire day, making them more productive in their work.

How Did I Come About the Morning Rituals?

I was not getting a proper solution to use my morning time efficiently. I was confused as to what time I should wake up. How many hours of sleep I should mandatorily take? If I slept fewer hours, I felt that waking up at the ring of the alarm clock would not freshen up my mind as my body did not get the required hours of sleep. I would snooze my alarm clock button and go back to sleep. Later on, after waking up, I would realize that I had wasted my day again. Further to my frustration of not waking up, I also felt guilty for not sticking to my routine which I had prepared a day before. These routines included walking, reading books, meditating, etc. My thoughts and plan remained on paper, which happened most of the time. It was giving me set back day by day. Still, I was curious to find the real technique of utilizing one hour after waking up in the morning so that I can take on any activity for the entire day. As you read this book, I am sure you will also be going through the same phase, and this happens not only to you but to most of the people who want to become morning people but cannot achieve their goals. I congratulate you for purchasing this book as I can assure you that this dilemma will now be over once and for all. You have purchased this book and reached up to this page, which proves that you want to change your lifestyle and achieve the dreams of your choice. I was always looking for a solution to improve my lifestyle, inculcate good waking habits and utilize the morning hours most beneficially. I had always wanted to be a morning person who ritually sticks to waking up early and feeling energized for the entire day. There was a fire within me to best utilize the morning hours and maintain the consistency of my early waking-up habit. I have researched many books on morning habits to make morning waking a daily ritual. Some books talked about the activities you prefer to be done in the morning based on your liking which may be meditating, reading books, listening to soothing music, running, walking etc. But I was not getting the solution I wanted to kickstart my day. I read many books, listened to many Ted talks on morning habits, and finally, I could merge various concepts after experimenting with various permutations and combinations on me to form a set of morning habits that changed my life. I have been following these morning rituals for the past five years, and I strongly recommend adopting these rituals, which have changed my life.

I have devised strategic time-bound morning activities one after the other for 60 minutes that set the tone for the day. The activities re-energize and revitalize me and make me feel at the top of the world. After my morning activities, I feel highly confident, with all thoughts aligned properly for the entire day. My face gets a radiance with a positive outlook, and I am ready to accept any task for the day. My memory power and my intelligence to grab any subject have improved. In this journey, I have also treasured the secret of learning conceptually any subject which may be strange to me. I will reveal the secret to the entire universe in my next book, which on practicing, will lead you to become a learned personality in any subject, a personality which you have never imagined. Yes, I can vouch that the secret is that strong. But to achieve that, you must first become a morning person by practicing the techniques taught in this book. I want my readers to achieve their first level of success. I guarantee that you will be a changed person and achieve health, wealth, prosperity, and happiness. I have done it and achieved it, and still, I am achieving more.

The first principle to start the journey is to forget about your past, who you were, and what you did earlier. Every day is a new day, and it starts today. The book "Awaken the Giant Inside," by Anthony Robbins says that you are what you decide now and can transform yourself. The only mantra is to take a "Decision" and then see the changes this decision will bring in your life. People are in the habit of procrastinating, pulling themselves down, and slowly losing their self-confidence. They don't take decisions, and if they do, they don't remain firm. The first key to success is taking decisions, followed by the habit you must stick to in order to witness the fruits of the decision. Research tells us that if any activity is performed for a continuous 21 days, it becomes a habit, and eventually, after 21 days, one starts enjoying the new habit. I guarantee that once you cross 21 days, you cannot live without those habits. I will discuss in the chapters the morning rituals based on habits you must follow for 21 days. After 21 days, you can find the difference. You will be amazed to find yourself improving in all areas in whichever phase of life you are, whether you are a student, a professional, homemaker, a businessperson etc. This morning ritual is for everyone, and one can easily imbibe it and get a transformed life. You know what? Life is beautiful, and we should enjoy life by taking advantage of the full potential of mind and body. Once you control your mind and body, you can achieve anything extraordinary. So, let's start learning. A learning journey that is going to transform your life forever. Whatever techniques I am going to talk about are not only the techniques I have assimilated from various sources but also, I have experienced them. I will tell you about each technique in detail in the subsequent chapters. I have applied those techniques to myself and found a dramatic change within me. First and foremost, start with your sleeping habits.

How much sleep is required?

I have researched several articles on the optimum hours of sleep required, but I could not find the answer. Based on the various articles I have read, I did multiple experiments on myself by sleeping early and resting for 7 hours, 8 hours and even for 9 hours. Sleeping to what extent is important is always a question in the mind of everyone. I am sure these thoughts might be going through your thought process as well as how many hours to sleep because many times if you sleep late, you do not feel fresh in the morning. The entire day you feel lazy. But the question is whether this is a roadblock in our minds. Whether our mind should witness 7 or 8 hrs of sleep and only then we can feel fresh in the morning. You will not agree with me now. Once you go through the chapters you will understand the science of feeling energetic. I have interacted with many people and asked how many hours of sleep they need. I get the answer in the range of 7hrs-8hrs, and some even say 9 hrs. But when I ask them, do you feel fresh after waking up? I get a mixed reply. Some say yes, and some say it depends on sleep quality. But then I also ask them if they feel energetic the whole day and have good vibes and thoughts for performing their work in the office or business. Few are sure, but few are unsure of where their life is taking them. They are just flowing wherever life takes them. In the book "Awaken the Giant Inside", Anthony Robbins said that for most people, their life is like a free boat moving in the direction of a stream of water. Wherever the stream is taking the boat, the boat is moving, but at one point, when the sudden steep creeks come, the boat goes along with the water flow and falls into the creek. This is dangerous. Similarly, people take their lives. Their lives move like the boat moving with the flow of a stream. They don't take charge of their life of which they are capable. They can change the direction of their life with just one decision to change their life for the better like using the oars. The direction of the boat can be changed, and the boat can be moved to a pleasant place where one can see more greenery and enjoy the surroundings. This example calls for immediate taking control of our life, and each of us can do it.

Life is wonderful, but the only essential is to know the technique of enjoying life. I will tell you how to enjoy life and take full advantage of life. Each one of the readers here is blessed to have a beautiful life. Life of your dreams. A life on your terms. A life of financial freedom. A life of abundance and wealth. A life of good health, and I guarantee that once you follow the techniques given in the book- you will be amazed to find a dramatic improvement in yourself. Yes, you can and have the inherent potential to do that. All the techniques I will discuss in this book are straightforward and do not require spending any amount. It is simply maintaining consistency in your morning ritual habits that you must perform in your Victory Hour. The only commitment I want from you is to follow the Morning Victory Hour habits in true spirit and not miss a day practicing those techniques.

Some readers may think they are night owls and can't wake up in the morning. They have been sleeping very late in the night for so many years and will find it hard to suddenly break that chronic habit. The answer is you can with just one decision of waking up early in the morning no matter when you sleep. It is a hard decision, but it will bring you positive results. The following quote of Boxing Champion Muhammad Ali will inspire you **"I hated every minute of training, but I said," Don't quit.**

Suffer now and live the rest of your life as a champion."

One should always take a cue from the universe to lead a beautiful life. The way the universe operates for the entire 24 hours from the rising sun to sunset to night. Similarly, our body is made on certain principles and follows the universe's clock. The universe, if you observe minutely, teaches us a lot. The rising of the sun and the setting of the sun have a fixed time. When the sun rises, a beautiful morning starts with sun rays becoming brighter and brighter, and all living beings are expected to start their day and get busy in their activities. After sunset, the sun's rays slowly dimmer, and the same bright day becomes dark, indicating that living beings should start settling for rest and sleep. Universe has set the timetable of daytime for work and night for sleeping. This is the first principle on which the learnings of this book are based. Some readers might think that because of their office work they have to work late at night and then how do they wake up in the morning? Don't worry. This book is for everyone, and the techniques taught do not impress upon seven or eight hours of sleep. It teaches you to energize yourself for the whole day by practicing the laid-down techniques after you wake up. You must "Grab your victory hour" after you wake up and follow the rituals taught in the book to become more productive in your work, achieve your dreams, and succeed in any field you desire. You become extraordinary by practicing the techniques for 60 minutes daily. Enjoy your learning journey.

May I ask you a small favor

I would love to know your thoughts on this book. I would be all ears to your feedback because I am eager to find ways to improve. I will listen to negative comments with an open mind and try to fix your concern. Drop me an email at gyansnarayan22@gmail.com.

I look forward to hearing from you. Also, if you liked this book, don't forget to leave a review. It will help the world become a more productive place.

Acknowledgement

I thank my parents, who have inculcated in me a good habit of reading books, making this book compilation possible for you. I am highly indebted to my wife, Sanchita, who always encouraged me to write the learnings I practice by listening to various podcasts and reading self-help books for the betterment of the readers. This book would not have been possible without her support and the sacrifices she made at weekends allowing me to write the book in solitude. I would also like to acknowledge the sacrifice made by my little daughter, Ishanvi, as she did not demand to play with me whenever she found me writing the manuscript. I love both of them.

Copyright

Disclaimer

The information given in this book is based on the research done by the author and is not intended or implied to be a substitute for professional medical advice. All content, including text, graphics, images and information contained on or available through this book is for general information purposes only.